Crazy in

Are we all crazy?

An introduction to a society besieged with
mental illness and a simpler way to deal with life….
By Lola Carlile, Ph.D.

Lola Carlile is an art therapist trained in psychotherapy and is the director of Masabi (Mind and Spirit and Body Improvement), providing expressive arts therapy to women, children, families, and the elderly.

She received her Master's degree in Art Therapy Counseling from Marylhurst University in Oregon in 2011. Her previous experience includes teaching all grades (preschool through the university level). She received her doctorate in education from The University of Texas at Austin in 1993.

She lives in the Northwest with her husband of 40+ years and is the mother of three grown sons. She has one precious granddaughter and one beloved grandson.

Are We All Crazy?

Lola Carlile, M.Ed., Ph.D.

Are We All Crazy?

Lola Carlile, Ph.D.

MASABI PRESS
Publisher
PO Box 2663, Salem, Oregon, 97308, USA

Printed by www.createspace.com 5/27/2013

ISBN-13:
978-1505233650

ISBN-10:
1505233658

Dedication

For Janell and Sandy who supported the idea of this book at its inception

For my dear Mother (and sister and brother) who suffered tremendous stress and kept on going despite the pain

And to all the children and adults who touched my heart as we experienced art and healing together

Contents

Introduction

The Sea of Insanity

Being fully awake in a global lunatic asylum is enough to make a person go insane. It feels like I'm stranded on an isolated island with a handful of traumatized survivors, surrounded by a sea of sadomasochists, homicidal maniacs and delusional cult members. The lifeboats have all sunk. On the other hand, if the world was as we know it should be, there would be so little drama as to render it mundane. I just wish it was "less" insane. The insanity seems to give my life meaning. And the hopeless situation teaches the lesson of acceptance. Acceptance would be a difficult lesson to learn in a world without the cult like insanity of statism.

Libertarian Blog

After living on this earth more than five decades, it has come to my attention that most of us are mentally unwell. In this advanced and progressive western society, mental illness can be a misnomer. Are we all ill? Or are our symptoms descriptive of the old bell curve? No one is truly normal. Are we all simply crazy? What is the new normal? And what is not?

About seven years ago I took an informal survey of individuals with whom I worked and 99% of them were on valium, Xanax, or some other anxiety-reducing pharmaceutical.

Stress is everywhere you look. We wake up in the morning stressed about the weather, what to wear, what to eat, and how to do what we need to do. Instead of a limited palette, we thrive on a complex series of events which are sure to create a dull form of stress – a stress that is inevitably going to cause us more trouble than we can imagine. This negative stress is referred to as distress. It is dangerous and we all succumb to its power.

Is stress indigenous to our society? History shows that stress for humans has been a constant since the inception of our kind. We only need to look at stories from the Bible and Adam and Eve - now there's stress at its finest. *Don't eat the fruit of the tree or else!* Temptation, disobedience, and more – all in one story.

As I began to look upon my life and examine the stressors, I wish I had the skills I now hold earlier in my life. I could have helped my stressed family members who just let it all out – never filtering an emotion.

I would probably not have yelled so much at my sons in high school nor would I have made myself miserable every time someone did something wrong, mean, or disrespectful to me. I should have learned from my dear husband whose philosophy is: *If someone calls me a name, I look at it two ways. If I am what they say, they are right. If I am not, then they are wrong. Period.*

It is true that this man is seemingly unstressed as he goes about life. He is unstressed about things that would send me through the roof, but I am gradually teaching myself to think the same way. What others say or do should not interfere with my happiness. What a novel idea.

The format of this book is workbook style. As an art therapist, I cannot fathom just reading and not doing as one reads. So during parts of the book you are asked to reflect and write and/or draw. These tasks are not mandatory (perish the thought), but will actually enable you to think on a different plane and to extend your understanding.

And, so, dear reader, I am sharing some amazing ways to deal with stress other than let it fester and eat you up from the inside. If you take the time to journey with me, you will see that no matter what the situation, you can control **YOU**. The end. Nothing else. You can only control **YOU** and the sooner you realize that fact, the better your life will be. And if you think you are normal and just need a skill set to understand Auntie Jane, then this book is for you, too. Are you ready to move on?

Bring your baggage with you....but be prepared to part with most of it. Enter the journey of healing....Not only will you learn about mental illness, but you will also understand how to heal, deal, and live with a mental illness in a positive and proactive manner.

Chapter 1

What is crazy?

"Lunatics are similar to designated hitters. Often an entire family is crazy, but since an entire family can't go into the hospital, one person is designated as crazy and goes inside. Then, depending on how the rest of the family is feeling that person is kept inside or snatched out, to prove something about the family's mental health."

Susanna Kaysen

We hear it all the time. *She's just crazy! You know he is crazy – leave him alone. Girl, you are cra-zee!* But what exactly is crazy? And whose definition are we going by? According to the Merriam-Webster dictionary online, **CRAZY** is defined in four ways:

1. mentally deranged, esp. as manifested in a wild or aggressive way.
"Stella **went crazy** and assaulted a visitor."

2. extremely enthusiastic.
"I'm **crazy about** Cindy."

3. appearing absurdly out of place or in an unlikely position.
"The monument leaned at a crazy angle."

4. a mentally deranged person.

The definition most of us really are referring to is either number 2 or 3; however, what most of us are hearing is number 1 or 4. The stigma of being labeled crazy or mentally ill is still alive and well in our culture and number 1 or 4 are not amusing nor desirable traits to possess.

Just try telling a possible employer during an interview that you have a mental illness. The likelihood of getting that job is slimmer than you thought now that you have broached the topic of mental illness. Yes, we know that employers cannot discriminate based on mental illness, but how is one able to prove that discriminatory act?

One in four Americans suffer from a diagnosable mental illness in any given year. In 2004 more than 57 million individuals were diagnosed with a mental illness. Locate three friends and include yourself in that group. One of you may have a mental illness! Is it you?

The good news is that only one in seventeen individuals with mental illness are severe enough that they require hospitalization, account for disability claims, and need more extensive care. The rest of us deal with our afflictions with self-remedies, occasional therapy, possibly medication, and alternative forms of therapy, such as meditation, religion, yoga, massage, acupuncture, and the expressive arts.

The day may come for us when we have to step up the care a notch. We all have the propensity to become ill and sometimes it takes a trigger in our life to lead us to that place.

Crazy little things crop up on our lives and sometimes we don't even know how they got there. For instance, when I was a little girl, I remember not wanting to step on a crack or it might do something to my mother. Now I knew in my head that Mama would not get a broken back should I step on a crack, but deep down inside I thought maybe something would happen to her. So I nervously avoided those stupid cracks!

Sounds like the beginning of some anxiety ridden tic or phobia or disorder....or something equally disturbing, right?

Then there was the time when I was in high school and I feared death so much. I remember not ever wanting children because why in the world would someone have kids just to know that they would have to face dying someday? It really, as they say, freaked me out.

I wrote poems about death, even organized a mini course on death at the local Catholic Church and still feared it. Even today I am not a fan of death.

We all have fears and only when they become so all-encompassing and so all-consuming that we declare that they are mental disorders.

Think of someone you know who is mentally ill or you think may be so. Draw a comic illustrating traits you believe make that person mentally ill. List the reasons why you believe that person is ill.

Van Gogh was mentally ill. We frequently hear that he was crazy. How does one distinguish between crazy and genius? Between mental illness and genius? Is it possible to do so?

Interestingly, on an online psychiatric group, one individual commented, "Maybe this is me being crazy, but I believe that many of today's mental 'illnesses' are unlikely to be illnesses at all, and that it is more likely that our current take on reality is the thing that is 'ill', with accepted thought patterns that are almost entirely scientific, linear, empirical. What has happened to thought patterns that are panoramic, far-reaching, metaphors? It does seem as though pure scientific thought has become the norm, but thinking in metaphor has now become crazy."

Thought patterns in our society have changed. What was once considered normal is now viewed as not normal. Shamans and revered prophets of the past who saw visions were respected. In today's world, someone who has visions is seen as schizophrenic and crazy. The PC world comes apart at the seams when one writes about crazy, but that is the vernacular of the common folk and one we hear most often.

And that is where education enters. When we see someone acting crazy, posing a threat to others, then our mindset must be that individual is ill and needs help. Crazy, if you will, but nevertheless, needing compassion and assistance.

Personally, I've been called crazy more than a few times. I've learned that those who call me that are not doing so in malice, but in frustration with my emotional self. And I have learned that I can indeed change my attitude and beliefs by studying them *if* I so desire.

I was raised with very few affective filters. If I felt mad, I yelled. If I was hurt, I cried. In short, if I felt it, I showed it. I was like an open book or maybe more akin to the critters we keep as pets.

I never realized I could change this. I did not have to be a walking talking drama machine, nor did I want to be that way anymore. My journey towards a healthier me spans more than six decades and is still a work in progress.

So am I crazy? Am I mentally ill? Where do I fit on the scale of mental health and mental illness? Am I sometimes a bit crazy? You bet! Put me with someone who is controlling and angry and you will see crazy. I might cry, talk rapidly, and become a bit paranoid. But now that I know what may trigger my feelings, I can begin to change them.

So what are your triggers? What makes you mad or sad? Are you tired of feeling too emotional? Do you really want to change? This is the day you can begin to create a new and healthier you. On the next page, draw some of the triggers that create frustration for you. Loud noises? Someone cutting in front of you in the grocery?

Draw the things that make you mad and sad and think of how you react to those triggers.

Pick one trigger. Imagine someone honking at you in traffic. What is your usual reaction? Speed up and cut them off? Flip them off? Honk your horn? Or do nothing? If you ignore the abuser, you are practicing good mental health. If you react with equal venom, then you are in for problems. Because each time you react violently it becomes easier to react that way the next time.

For example, when I taught 8th grade English and we were studying racism, I had a poem I wanted to read to the students. It had the **N** word in it. I had never used that word before and it felt awful to read it. I could have glossed over it, but I explained to my students that they would not get the true feel for what happened if I substituted the word, so I read the poem with the word intact. It felt absolutely dreadful as I did so first period as well as for the next two classes. But by the seventh period, it didn't feel that bad! I explained this phenomenon to the students and shared why bad habits are not so easily shed. The more we do something, the easier it becomes. It then becomes a habit, albeit a bad one at times. So if we react a certain way continuously, it then becomes a habit. Breaking habits becomes far more arduous than creating them.

But before you can break a bad habit, you have to realize it is a bad habit. How you react to other people's anger can and should be changed if your response is equally angry on a consistent basis.

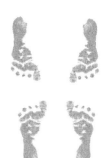

Baby steps is what we do. We know that we have a behavior we need to change. Now we are ready to change it, but how?

Relax. Stay calm and look at your triggers. How can you react in a less stressful way?

Chapter 2

Types of Crazy

"Our society tends to regard as a sickness any mode of thought or behavior that is inconvenient for the system and this is plausible because when an individual doesn't fit into the system it causes pain to the individual as well as problems for the system. Thus the manipulation of an individual to adjust him to the system is seen as a cure for a sickness and therefore as good."

Theodore Kaczynski

A buffet of symptoms arise when someone is diagnosed with a mental illness. These range from being having depressive and anxious feelings to deep, dark feelings of despair and guilt. The gamut of symptoms fill an entire book (The Diagnostic and Statistical Manual of Mental Disorders Fifth Edition – the DSM) – almost 1,000 pages, so it is no wonder people are in the dark about mental illness.

What may have been abnormal when I started studying psychology in the 1960s is now perfectly acceptable! In those days we were taught that homosexuality was an aberrant behavior. Today the PC police have ensured that the public sees this lifestyle as an alternative way of living and that belief is reflected in the current DSM 5 text. Who knows what we think is abnormal today might very well be thought of as perfectly normal in the future. Psychology is truly a cultural and emotional study; whereas, medicine tends to be more scientific. Cancer is cancer throughout the world. It is possible to cure it with certain medications, procedures, etc. But certain symptoms pointing to mental illness may not really be cured or changed or even considered a sickness. And each symptom can be physical, mental, or a combination of both.

Many individuals claim that psychiatry is a soft science – one that lacks empirical evidence. If I break my arm, you can see the break on an x ray. If my mind is broken, you can't visibly *SEE* it. I can be in a coma and you can still tell if I have a broken limb or problem with my heart. But if I am psychotic and in a coma, you might never know….

That being said, how many symptoms and how severe must they be for an individual to take notice and/or seek professional assistance? Perhaps the following analogy will help.

George is finicky. He picks at his food. When his mother reminds him to eat, he yells and throws his eating utensils. His mother can't remember a time when George was not a difficult child. Her life is miserable. George has no friends. The children in his second grade classroom are afraid of him. The teacher is at her wits' end. Obviously, this is a problem child who needs testing and observation and some professional help.

On the other hand, after interviewing George's mom, it is evident that she also reacts to others in a defiant and negative manner. Has George learned this behavior? Can mental illness be a learned behavior? Even if George has learned this behavior, he still needs intervention to overcome the negativity of such defiance.

It is evident that the entire family needs counseling. Negative and/or bad learned behavior needs to be unlearned and it takes that proverbial village to raise a child. The entire nuclear family needs to understand what is not working and how to change it in order to create a harmonious relationship within the family nucleus as well as the community, including the school arena.

Is mental illness contagious? In a sense, one might say yes. Mimicry is how we learn. We imprint our parents' behavior onto our own. If no one makes a correction, then that behavior simply continues throughout the lifetime of that child.

With that said, the book that is the bible of the psychiatric world is called the DSM-5 (the IV is now put to rest). It is short for Diagnostic and Statistical Manual. This manual is for therapists and psychiatrists and lists every possible *CURRENT* mental illness. Mind you, I said current. In the past, several symptoms and syndromes were thought of as mental illness, but today the PC police would slap you on the wrist if you referred to those behaviors as mental illnesses.

Autism is a word most people are aware of and most individuals think of it as a social malady; however, autism is now reflected and grouped with Asperger's (think Sheldon on *The Big Bang Theory),* and now instead of calling someone mentally retarded, the current label is intellectual disability. I would imagine the highly educated doctors of psychiatry who oversee and wrote the DSM-5 would absolutely cringe at the way we are using the word crazy here. Absolutely not PC!

If you are interested in how psychiatry is changing, just go to this link and if you are able to plow through the lengthy and wordy document, you will see changes that have been made to the illnesses we suspect may be mental illness.

http://psychology.about.com/od/psychotherapy/f/faq_dsm.htm

Anytime you have a symptom of something, you can probably find a syndrome or disease it might be. A curious phenomenon happens to doctors in medical school. They begin to experience symptoms of diseases they study. Not to be outdone by the doctors of the day, when we studied psychiatry, I was sure I was a walking demo for many of the illnesses. Or, if I wasn't, surely someone in my family was! So the point here is that when you read about the illnesses in the DSM-5, don't fall for that same syndrome – self-diagnosis might be dangerous to your health. A professional needs to do it.

One big change is to drop the Axes that the therapist used to evaluate and diagnose an individual's illness. Now there are twenty some disorders to use. No longer are addictions called so – now they are disorders.

If you continually pick at your skin, there is a diagnosis for you. If you are grieved when Grandma dies and just can't get over it, there is a diagnosis for you. If your five-year old is combative and difficult to control, there is a diagnosis for him or her….

Not to make light of mental illness, I want to make it perfectly clear that we are a race of imperfections. It is only when these problems interfere with daily work and life is it a problem that needs attention by a professional.

What does it matter if you have a psychiatric diagnosis? According to Baumann (2002), "the main function is to provide a succinct and consistent means of communicating a large amount of information about a client's illness."

So who has a need to know? Your physician. Your drug company. Your family. You.

On the next page, draw what you think might be of concern about you or something that you do or think that just is giving you reason to worry….or do the same about someone you worry.

WORRIES....Draw or write for the next few pages....

How do you deal with these worries?

List all possible ways with which to deal with these worries.

What do you think would happen if you shared with your doctor?

Chapter 3

Insidious Anxiety

Some of your hurts you have cured,
And the sharpest you still have survived,
But what torments of grief you endured
From the evil which never arrived.

Ralph Waldo Emerson

I became so anxious when I wrote this chapter the first time, I lost it. Seriously. Lost it. Could not find it, although the rest of the manuscript was intact, including chapter 4. Freudian something or the other must have been to blame.

Speaking of Freud, studying about Freudian psychology can cause immense tension in the tender hearted. So if my son hugs me too long does that mean he wants to marry me? Maybe he just loves his mother. Oh, but I digress. I need to emphasize that I may sound light hearted when it comes to talking about mental health, but taking it all too seriously creates copious amounts of stress in individuals that can certainly lessen the quality of their lives.

An avid Facebook fan, I found several self-help and moral support groups for a variety of mental illnesses. On the anxiety group I found many very willing to laugh with me and agree that maybe we are all crazy. They even agreed with the title of the book. Sometimes we have become so serious that we create our own hell in our head.

Cath says, "I use tarot images, or art cards, story therapy techniques to build a narrative. Had a client once who could not cross a bridge, it was a good way to deflect the anxiety and it worked for her."

The imagery in art can indeed become healthy.

Anxiety can be controlled and we can learn to do so by using a method called *cognitive behavioral therapy.* As I've mentioned before (or if I haven't, I have wanted to!), we are in control of our emotions. We can control how we perceive any action, word, or deed outside of ourselves. First of all, we need to want to do so. Secondly, we must recognize our behavior and then learn what triggers or causes this behavior. Then we can decide how we WANT to behave or think when this same trigger occurs again in our lives. It's really simple, but takes a while. I usually tell my clients it takes about 3 – 4 months to learn the process and practice it, but the longer we are in control of our emotions, the better the outcome for us.

Anxiety is described by one young woman as a "chill moving slowly up my body to my brain where I feel I must blink a thousand times to rid myself of the negativity and angst. Then my heart begins to palpitate quickly and so loudly that I hear the blood pulsing throughout my body. I know that if I do not do something quickly, I will have a full-blown anxiety attack. I never knew I could control this phenomenon."

It is indeed a relief to know that we need no longer suffer from anxiety. We can control it if that is our desire.

Take a moment to just scribble. Close your eyes, hold the pencil or pen and make some lines on paper. Look at it. Turn it around and look some more. What do you see? Do you see anything? Color your scribble. That simple pleasure of coloring is something we as adults forget all too soon. This simple act allows us to focus and rid ourselves, albeit temporarily, of stress and angst. Done more often, we can keep our negativity at bay for longer periods of time.

Chapter 4

Dealing with Depression

"The best thing for being sad," replied Merlin, beginning to puff and blow, "is to learn something. That's the only thing that never fails. You may grow old and trembling in your anatomies, you may lie awake at night listening to the disorder of your veins, you may miss your only love, you may see the world about you devastated by evil lunatics, or know your honour trampled in the sewers of baser minds. There is only one thing for it then — to learn. Learn why the world wags and what wags it. That is the only thing which the mind can never exhaust, never alienate, never be tortured by, never fear or distrust, and never dream of regretting. Learning is the only thing for you. Look what a lot of things there are to learn."
T.H. White, *The Once and Future King*

Depression is defined by the Mayo Clinic as a *medical illness that causes a persistent feeling of sadness and loss of interest. It can also cause physical symptoms.* Everyone kind of understands that people generally can and do get depressed. Things such as losing your job can make you depressed. Not having enough money at the end of the month can also cause depression. Many things create sadness and depression in our society, so when is depression a medical illness and when does it need to be treated by a health professional?

It is helpful to know that depression is not something you can **SNAP** out of or something that will go away without intervention. Depression can create physical problems, a feeling that life is not worth living, and cause many more emotional problems.

Is there a cure? Definitely! With proper medication or therapy or a combination of both, individuals can manage their depression and perform their day to day activities with freedom from sadness that permeates their lives.

People deal with depression in many ways, one of which is self-talk. When I become sad and start to cry, I ask myself if this is really something about which to cry? If it is, I cry and then that's it. If I continue crying, I try to distract myself with something I love or like or used to enjoy.

Maybe it's some beautiful music or a memory of something of which I am fond . . . making art helps tremendously because it focuses your brain and allows you to find peace and relaxation. One of my favorite sites online is adult coloring (don't worry, it's not R rated!) and I print out a sheet and color it to my heart's desire. The very motion of using a thin marker or a colored pencil moving back and forth is soothing and allows your senses to be calmed. You will find a series of art activities to do at the end of this book. If you don't think you are a good artist or haven't formerly liked art, you may be surprised at the variety offered.

Sometimes I just pick up a pencil and scribble. Then I fill in the page with color. Very relaxing and afterwards I can toss it or keep it as a reminder of what helped me cheer up.

http://www.coloring-pages-for-all-ages.com/adult-coloring-pages.html

Art is not the only healing phenomenon. Music, drama, dance, or anything that takes your mind off you will work. Various forms of art also help soothe the soul, such as sewing, wood working, crochet, and so on. You get the idea – be creative and get working so that your mind does not have time to tempt and taunt you into depressive bouts.

Not all art activities are suitable for everyone. Recently one of my favorite pages lay upon my desk. Both my brother and husband commented that coloring that - even looking at it - made them nervous! So different strokes for some folks…

Scribbling! Take a sheet of paper and pencil and scribble to your heart's desire. Then color it in. Take a deep breath. Ahh…Do you feel the stress and depression lifting? ☺

Folks can achieve a lift in life by DBT (Dialectical Behavioral Therapy). This strategy involves awareness of the moment. Some people refer to it as *being in the moment*, in addition to other strategies.

Oftentimes depression leads people to wander and wail in the past. Would have, should have, could have….we can't change the past, so we must realize that we can only live in the present. Sure, it's okay to think about the past once in a while, but to live there and not live in the present can create stress and depression.

With DBT individuals learn about mindfulness, interpersonal communication, distress tolerance, and emotional regulation. A series of sessions usually lasts 8 - 10 weeks. Some people require a longer time period to learn healthy techniques and thinking processes. You've probably heard the saying *It Is What It Is.* That sort of describes DBT.

What are some thoughts you have that cause you sorrow? Draw or write them here. Then think of a way to change that mindset.

Depression can vary with the seasons as well. It may flare up due to physical ailments, sun or absence thereof, lack of sleep or good nutrition, or a combination of any of the above. It also occurs when we become so inward centered that we almost order it to appear!

Research has shown the "religious" people tend to feel less depression. Why could that be? Could it be that the religious individual is taught to think of others, to give to others, and to love others? The depressed person is only thinking of others in relation to him or herself. How is this affecting me? How do I feel about this?

When I was growing up the adage *idleness is the devil's workshop* was the refrain of many a parent. Keep those kids busy and they will be happy. Truer words were never spoken.

My own mother signed me up to volunteer to teach English to Cuban refugee teens when I was a freshman and sophomore in high school. She strongly supported me babysitting whenever I had the time. She was a wise woman. I was rarely depressed in my early and mid-teens.

When I stopped my altruistic endeavors and began working and thinking about myself and my wants, I went through a period of complete depression where I wrote dark poetry and thought often of death.

The cycle of depression is very difficult to break. The fact that I wrote about death actually helped me to not become as depressed. I remember one counselor told me to write about my hypochondria. He told me that perhaps I could help others. Sure enough, I started writing a column for a local newspaper and my hypochondria started to melt away. It took a long time, but it did eventually go away. That was one smart counselor!

The way we can stop this destructive cycle of depression is to recognize the triggers. What is it that makes us start to become depressed? Is it loneliness? If so, when we start to fidget and think we are lonely, we need to do something to fight that loneliness. Maybe it is calling someone on the phone. Maybe it is going on Facebook and connecting with others from the confines of their homes. Maybe it's going for a walk in the mall. Whatever works for you to get out of the feeling sorry for yourself mode.

The moment we come home from that excursion, it is possible we start thinking again about some other trigger. We have to be constantly vigilant and ready to stomp on those negative thoughts and change them to healthier manifestations of our souls.

It won't happen overnight. It won't happen in a few weeks, but it will get better and eventually eradicate chronic depression if we continue monitoring our moods and making positive changes in our thought patterns.

Chapter 5

Autism Uncovered

I think that people with autism are born outside the regime of civilization. Sure, this is just my own made-up theory, but I think that, as a result of all the killings in the world and the selfish planet-wrecking that humanity has committed, a deep sense of crisis exists. Autism has somehow arisen out of this. Although people with autism look like other people physically, we are in fact very different in many ways. We are more like travelers from the distant, distant past. And if, by our being here, we could help the people of the world remember what truly matters for the Earth that would give us a quiet pleasure."

> Naoki Higashida, The Reason
> I Jump: The Inner Voice of a
> Thirteen-Year-Old Boy with
> Autism

Autism is a *yuppy* disease, some folks say. Autism encompasses what we used to say were the mentally retarded, the gifted, and the odd. Very un-PC!

Autism is manifested by three characteristics: social, communication, and behavior. Several screening tests are available to screen for autism. One is the ADOS - Autism Diagnostic Observation Scale. This checklist is considered the gold standard for diagnosing autism and is used by professionals only; however, there is hope and the link

http://www.autismspeaks.org/what-autism/diagnosis/screen-your-child

allows parents to screen their child(ren) and then refer the results to their physician as needed. Amazingly, many resources are available to those identified as autistic.

The scale of mild to severe autism is as varied as the pebbles on the beach. Most children diagnosed as autistic can be efficient and productive citizens in our society.

The diagnostic screening tool available for parents seems to be on the restrictive side for a friend completed it for her oldest son who is now 35 and amazingly successful, married, a father, and in the military. He is extremely intelligent and the screening tool indicated he was at **mild** risk of autism.

His pediatricians never questioned his development nor did his parents, so with this in mind, it is often wise for a parent to go with their gut feeling. You know when something is not right with your child, so keep up with regular medical checkups and be communicative with your physician.

Fortunately, my friend's gut feeling was that her child was exceptional in the fact that he was brilliant. When he was less than three years old, he ran into the house, proclaiming, *Mama, mama, when I hold my finger in the air, I can feel the direction of the wind.* You can draw your own conclusions.

I have several friends who lovingly refer to their children and/or spouses as *slightly Asperger's.* This term is applied to assuage the feelings that sometimes people are rude, thoughtless, and forgetful. It is not always the case that the individual can be excused for his or her lack of civility.

Truly autistic individuals cannot help their behavior quirks and only with the assistance of qualified health professionals can learn to navigate in this societal tempest.

What are the recognized symptoms that may indicate a diagnosis of autism? For you television savvy guys, just watch one episode of *The Big Bang Theory.* Oh, my, Sheldon is the poster child for Asperger's which is on the autism scale. I don't care what the producers and writers say! Very smart, but missing something on the social scene....

Draw what you think an autistic child's mind might look like....

Chapter 6

Behavioral Disorders

Those kids really drove me crazy today. I started getting cramps and almost had to leave the classroom. Why do they have to act out so? I wonder if their regular teacher has better control of their behavior?

Classroom sub

After teaching more than three decades, I can honestly say that I have probably seen more than my share of behaviorally challenged children (and some adults as well). They ran the gamut of having learning, social, and emotional problems.

Each child was different and probably symptoms in one child would be different than symptoms in another child. There is also the societal acceptance for what is "normal" behavior for each age group. This is where the classroom teacher (or homeschool mom) will have to be vigilant.

Although children can be screened at the physician's office, it is important to know that intervention strategies should be used before a child is referred to testing. Inappropriate behavior must be long-term and persistent in order to be classified as a disorder.

Some screening methods include IQ (intelligence) and achievement tests, interviews, self-evaluations, and direct behavioral observations.

If the behavior is pervasive enough, an Individualized Education Program (IEP) will be set up for the child. The child who is such labeled will receive special services at school, as well as home services if the child is homeschooled, depending on the state in which you live.

The cause of behavioral problems run the gamut from brain damage, physical illness or disabilities, malnutrition, genetics, and temperament.

Family factors that also contribute to such disorders are conflict, divorce, discipline style, coercion (nagging, threats, abuse), and inconsistent punishment. Parental behavior is also very important – language used at home (not as in English, etc.), attitudes towards authority, education, and school involvement all affect the behavior of children.

We all try to do the best we are able, but sometimes each family needs a little help. If assistance is sought out at first, it is more likely the child will be able to balance out his or her behavior.

Schools and personnel therein can have a definite effect on children. Staff must be aware of individual differences, have goals and expectations that are clear and reasonable, and use proper reinforcement and provide appropriate models of behavior. Schools must also be aware of developmentally appropriate learning and teaching strategies.

Many believe that a quiet classroom is a positive and functioning classroom when I know for a fact that is not the case. If in doubt about a class' efficacy for your child, simply go visit and watch the class in action. Your gut should tell you if this is an appropriate environment for your child.

Yes, my children watched television and probably more than they should have, but all grew up to be responsible and caring adults. Children who are already prone to violence, anger, and misbehavior, certainly don't need the negativity from television influencing their lives any more than possible.

Some labels we use to denote behavior disorders include conduct disorder, characterized by overt aggression, which may include lying, theft, arson, and "unmanageability." Boys are three times more likely as girls to have this disorder.

Symptoms to notice include change in school performance, withdrawal, change in personal appearance, mood swings, friends who seem wrong for your child (come on now, you know what I mean here), and changes in attitudes.

Some behavioral disorders are seemingly innocuous as they are not disruptive; however, they can be detrimental to learning. Self-esteem can be low and shyness and fearfulness increase. These children may be demonstrating signs of an anxiety disorder. Some signs include repeated actions (compulsions) and repeated thoughts (obsessions).

Children can learn to control these feelings by using CBT (cognitive behavioral therapy) as well – self-control training.

Hopefully, most of us parents have not had to deal with enuresis or encopresis. These terms apply to children who wet and/or soil themselves after the age of normal societal potty training age. This behavior can damage a child's self-image and severely limit the child's social acceptance.

Close monitoring and checking with the teacher, as well as working with the pediatrician to determine the cause of the problem is mandatory. It is also helpful for the child to be seen by a therapist for a while as well. The parent is responsible for gathering a support system for the child who is disturbed – pediatrician, therapist, and educators, as well as the parental units.

Think of a child whom you think may have behavioral problems. Write or draw what those behaviors are below. Did you have problems as a child? List them here. How have they changed for you?

Now take each one of those behaviors and determine if that behavior **can** be changed. How?

Chapter 7

Personality Disorders

Lost in the Maze

The mind of the girl we saw was a maze: Unbalanced, out-of-touch, Schizoid haze. Then she was me and I was the rat learning the maze: A mind like that. We studied her thoughts. We looked at her past. We took copious notes, From onset to last. I took their pills to offset the pain. Still, my mind was a haze and I hated my brain. She was a good study, an excellent case: Schizo-Affective Disorder at a rabid pace. I stared at nothing; it was easiest to do. I stopped calling friends, said I had the flu. She says she is dying, classic symptom that! She says there are voices and something about a rat...

Jai

This teen goes on to explain in her poem how she is in a maze that worsens and someday she will get lost and make the rat her pet. She comments on studies on the rat and how we are interested in the mind and how lonely it is to be sick in one's head – day after day....trying all the drugs and noting her progress, being watched for distress. She says she knows all the pills that are supposed to give her hope. But still she wants to die. She laughs, too, and tells us at the end of her poem that she is still lost in the maze and has given up hope for wellness and that the rat has died of exhaustion and hellishness.

The definition of a personality disorder, according to the Mayo Clinic is *a type of mental illness in which you have trouble perceiving and relating to situations and to people — including yourself. There are many specific types of personality disorders.*

In general, having a personality disorder means you have a rigid and unhealthy pattern of thinking and behaving no matter what the situation. This leads to

significant problems and limitations in
relationships, social encounters, work and school.

In some cases, you may not realize that you have a
personality disorder because your way of thinking
and behaving seems natural to you, and you may
blame others for the challenges you face.

Wait a minute here – that sounds like my entire
family and most of my friends! So how do we know
if we have a personality disorder? In the past we
simply said someone was weird, odd, selfish,
immature, crazy, or mad. Those are nice names. So
how does one ascertain when an individual is truly
suffering from a mental disorder?

According to the Mayo Clinic and not Wikipedia
(LOL), the following are symptoms of a personality
disorder:

- Frequent mood swings
- Stormy relationships
- Social isolation
- Angry outbursts

- Suspicion and mistrust of others
- Difficulty making friends
- A need for instant gratification
- Poor impulse control
- Alcohol or substance abuse

Hum, if I am honest about it, I can surely confirm that four of the nine could have applied to me at various times in my lifetime. How about you?

Well, then, what else do we need to know about personality disorders in order to discern a true mental illness? The Mayo Clinic spells it out for us in terms easy enough to understand, so read through these and check to see if you feel you or your loved ones seriously fall into one of these categories. If you do, go see a doctor soon!

The specific types of personality disorders are grouped into three clusters based on similar characteristics and symptoms. Many people with one diagnosed personality disorder also have signs and symptoms of at least one additional personality disorder.

Cluster A personality disorders
These are personality disorders characterized by odd, eccentric thinking or behavior and include:

Paranoid personality disorder
- *Distrust and suspicion of others*
- *Believing that others are trying to harm you*
- *Emotional detachment*
- *Hostility*

Schizoid personality disorder
- *Lack of interest in social relationships*
- *Limited range of emotional expression*
- *Inability to pick up normal social cues*
- *Appearing dull or indifferent to others*

Schizotypal personality disorder
- *Peculiar dress, thinking, beliefs or behavior*
- *Perceptual alterations, such as those affecting touch*

- *Discomfort in close relationships*
- *Flat emotions or inappropriate emotional responses*
- *Indifference to others*
- *"Magical thinking" — believing you can influence people and events with your thoughts*
- *Believing that messages are hidden for you in public speeches or displays*

Cluster B personality disorders
These are personality disorders characterized by dramatic, overly emotional thinking or behavior and include:

Antisocial (formerly called sociopathic) personality disorder
- *Disregard for others*
- *Persistent lying or stealing*
- *Recurring difficulties with the law*
- *Repeatedly violating the rights of others*
- *Aggressive, often violent behavior*
- *Disregard for the safety of self or others*

Borderline personality disorder
- *Impulsive and risky behavior*
- *Volatile relationships*
- *Unstable mood*
- *Suicidal behavior*
- *Fear of being alone*

Histrionic personality disorder
- *Constantly seeking attention*
- *Excessively emotional*
- *Extreme sensitivity to others' approval*
- *Unstable mood*
- *Excessive concern with physical appearance*

Narcissistic personality disorder
Believing that you're better than others
- *Fantasizing about power, success and attractiveness*
- *Exaggerating your achievements or talents*
- *Expecting constant praise and admiration*
- *Failing to recognize other people's emotions and feelings*

Cluster C personality disorders

These are personality disorders characterized by anxious, fearful thinking or behavior and include:

Avoidant personality disorder

- *Hypersensitivity to criticism or rejection*
- *Feeling inadequate*
- *Social isolation*
- *Extreme shyness in social situations*
- *Timidity*

Dependent personality disorder

- *Excessive dependence on others*
- *Submissiveness toward others*
- *A desire to be taken care of*
- *Tolerance of poor or abusive treatment*
- *Urgent need to start a new relationship when one has ended*

Obsessive-compulsive personality disorder
- *Preoccupation with orderliness and rules*
- *Extreme perfectionism*
- *Desire to be in control of situations*
- *Inability to discard broken or worthless objects*
- *Inflexibility*

Obsessive-compulsive personality disorder isn't the same as obsessive-compulsive disorder, a type of anxiety disorder.

I purposely used the Mayo Clinic's words verbatim. Why reinvent the wheel? And the checklists are so concise. The trouble is that we all can relate to one or more disorders.

When is our sadness truly a mental disorder? When is our jealous nature truly toxic and dangerous? That explains it.

Our personality characteristics are symptoms of mental illness when our lives and others are impaired. And not just for a day, but for a length of time.

We can retard the growth of mental illness if we recognize it in its infancy. We can learn to think more logically and heal ourselves. We can educate ourselves in order to prevent serious illness.

Sometimes.

Not always.

Some mental illnesses change the structure and chemical balance in our brains. When this occurs, we need medical help. A therapist who is worth her salt will refer an individual to a psychiatrist (medical doctor who diagnoses AND dispenses medication) for help in serious matters.
Sharlene was diagnosed with Borderline Personality Disorder. She says others have a hard time dealing with her diagnosis. She reports she is not getting better and has learned to just "deal with it." She

hasn't been able to find anyone to talk things out with – she had a new therapist (after her old one retired) and the new one repulsed her with comments that made Sharlene feel even worse. So her journey remains a struggle.

Yes, research has proven that good therapy can sometimes replace medication, and sometimes supplemented with medication, mental illness can be controlled and the individual can leave a happy and productive life. The goal of the team – therapists, doctors, and family – is to provide the least amount of assistance to provide the greatest level of healing.

Draw what sort of personality you have. Include the good and the not so helpful….What can you change? What should you keep just as it is?

Chapter 8

Mood Disorders

"If I can't feel, if I can't move, if I can't think, and I can't care, then what conceivable point is there in living?"

Kay Redfield Jamison

You've heard it many times: *She's such a bitch....*
Oh, he is moody…You never know which side of the
bed s/he is gonna wake up on!

Mood disorders are simply that: people fluctuate
between moods. Up, down, and all around. It is
normal to have a mood change. We can't be happy
all the time and we can't be sad all the time. I mean,
we can, but this state of change is not the norm. But
extremes and long lasting depression and/or mania
are causes for concern.

Welcome to my world! My family is known for its,
um, shall we say, emotional outbursts? If you are
mad, everyone knows it. If you are sad, same thing.
No filters. Learned behavior. And after decades,
many others flee when a change in mood begins to
percolate in one of my family members' façade. My
doctor cousin calls it the *family curse*.

We once sat down and named all the people in our
family we felt had it. Ironically, neither he nor I

named ourselves. We should have. We got it, too, sister! Yep, but through education and much practice, we have been able to subterfuge our moods. Don't be fooled, they are there, just waiting to explode in your face or anyone else's!

On some social media groups on the internet there are several groups for individuals suffering from mental illness. Many of these groups can be depressing in of themselves! Some groups are better than others and allow a commonality to bond individuals together and allow for additional healing.

Alyson shares the following:
I was diagnosed with BPD when I had a breakdown almost 10 years ago. I was prescribed a course of Cognitive Behavioral Therapy, which did nothing at all to help. In fact, it seemed to intensify my difficulties. I was prescribed a number of medications.. Seroxat (made me suicidal), Ativan (made me too sleepy to stand upright), Prothiadine

(made me very nauseous), Citralopram (no positive or negative effects) and Prozac.

Not all at the same time, just one after the other. I was getting nowhere and I could barely function.

My psychiatric doctor left the health service and I was teamed up with a new guy. This was over a period of three years and I was still functioning very poorly.

After spending only an hour with this lovely new man, he said I have BP disorder and prescribed me Depakote. Within two weeks I felt so much better.

There is hope to eradicate or lessen the effect of mental illness, but the same hope Alyson has is not the same other individuals have. Alyson is functioning well thanks to a physician and therapist who got it right. Many do not. The measure of success is how the individual is coping with life.

Gemma writes: *I have a temporary diagnosis of BPD which actually…fits me perfectly and I was weird realizing that some parts of me I hated were actually due to something and not just….me being a useless person. The only trouble with BPD is it doesn't cover a few main symptoms and I am waiting to see a specialist (sigh) and might get a diagnosis of DID, maybe even alongside BPD.*

I don't really mind the label, if anything, I appreciate it because with a label for it, I can get treatment and with a label, no doctor is going to tell me just to 'take it easy for a while' as a cure.

Gemma has also found appropriate treatment. She found solace in the fact that she had a name for her idea of just being "useless," a label possibly foisted on her by her family and friends and then embraced by her. She can now continue treatment and lead a fulfilling life in the near future.

Personality disorders are of concern as they are most difficult with which to deal, since they stem from experiences from childhood. Yes, people say, "Get over it! Grow up!" But it simply is not as easy as that.

Dr. Habid Sadeghi wrote a wonderful book entitled, "Within." In it he tries to share how to love oneself. If you do not love yourself, then you are not going to be as successful as you could be if you did. Seems like a no-brainer, eh?

This point of view does provide us with a schemata with which to look at life in a different way. For example, you have a person who is giving you grief – on and off type of love affair. It's driving you crazy, but if you think about it, the person offending you may simply not love him or herself, so feels the need to conflict others.

That bully down the street might possibly have a negative view of himself and is not able to love unconditionally. Those inner pains have to be dealt with in some way. Bullies attack others. Mean girls commit heinous little nasty acts to convolute the lives of others. Yet, their negative mannerisms are only symptoms of a greater ill—the one of not loving themselves enough to be kind and decent to themselves, as well as others.

I wish we were all trained to be parents – if I had known what I know now, I believe I would have been a happier and more productive parent. I did not realize that I could control my thoughts. I was raised with the notion that emotions ruled me!

Moody people oftentimes find themselves up one moment and down the next. But with a lot of effort and practice, that roller coaster of emotion can be controlled. When it is under control, the individual is most certainly experiencing a positive and fulfilling lifestyle.

Now that we are talking about moods, we also should be aware that our minds and bodies are intrinsically bound together. If we do not take care of our bodies, our minds will suffer.

Yo yo dieting and inconsistencies in our lives do not help our emotional well-being. Not eating a balanced diet is also quite detrimental to us, yet I have friends who have been "dieting" for 20+ years! Something is wrong there! What can we do? It is CRAZY – seriously, crazy, to be working on something for many years and never reach a goal.

The problem is that people don't hone in on everything to do with weight – you can't just change your diet – you have to think differently; you have to exercise; and you have to be consistent.

I am guilty of the above myself! When I tell myself I am going to diet, well, then, mister, you'd better believe I usually even gain weight! If I think I can't have something, then I want it all the more. That's crazy enough in of itself. . . .

In this age of instant gratification, we are used to getting what we want. If I want a new blouse, I jet on down to the mall and buy a blouse even if I don't have money. Why, I have a charge card, don't I? We want it and we want it now.

So we really are doing ourselves a disservice by granting our every wish. That's what parents do when they give their children everything they want. Why work for it when mommy and daddy will give it to me? That's where those basement boys come from – 30 something or others living in the basement of their parent's homes, not working, not going to school, but playing games and being eternal teens. It's our fault! We haven't taught the lesson of patience, working hard, and planning….

Whew! I got that one out pretty quickly, but you get the point. We respond to our wants so quickly that when we can't, we get depressed and, guess what? We are in for a moody day. . . .

That's partly why religions have sacrifices and prayers – so that people can realize they have to wait and have to sacrifice in order to achieve the ultimate goal – a lifetime resulting in finding Nirvana.

When was the last time you felt moody? Why? What caused it? How long did it last? When would that moodiness need a mental health practitioner to help? Draw or write your thoughts below.

Chapter 9

Schizophrenia

"Maybe each human being lives in a unique world, a private world different from those inhabited and experienced by all other humans. . . If reality differs from person to person, can we speak of reality singular, or shouldn't we really be talking about plural realities? And if there are plural realities, are some more true (more real) than others? What about the world of a schizophrenic? Maybe it's as real as our world. Maybe we cannot say that we are in touch with reality and he is not, but should instead say, His reality is so different from ours that he can't explain his to us, and we can't explain ours to him. The problem, then, is that if subjective worlds are experienced too differently, there occurs a breakdown in communication ... and there is the real illness."

Philip K. Dick

When I was doing my practicum in mental health counseling, I worked with a few groups of individuals diagnosed with schizophrenia. As I had very little experience with such people, I had no preconceived ideas of how they might be. I had sparse book knowledge, but little more than that.

At first, they appeared quite normal to me. In fact, I rarely saw any manifestations of their illnesses. My job was to give them a moment in time of peace, quiet, and positivity.

Until one young man asked me to please "tell the donkey to be quiet." To which I became startled and looked around, asking, "What donkey?"

He replied, "The one in my head. He is trying to make me do bad things."
My first inclination was wrong – it was to tell him that the donkey did not really exist.
Duly humbled by his response, I have frequently wondered how many times we belittle and/or deny

the realities of others just because we do not understand.

"Oh, yes, Lola! That donkey is real to **ME**!"

I shan't forget that moment ever. So, schizophrenia is a break from the expected and usual NORM.

If you want to see the poster child for schizophrenia, watch the film, "A Beautiful Mind." I actually ruined the movie for my husband and son, so will promise not to do so for you. Just rest assured that the film is amazing and shows what the world of a schizophrenic is like.

Schizophrenia is what most people really think of as crazy. These are people who may hear voices, have hallucinations, or believe others may be out to get them. These tortured individuals scare not only their families, but strangers as well. Are they violent? Can they turn on you?

About 1% of our population is diagnosed with schizophrenia. And many lead productive and normal lives with appropriate medication and therapy.

They can become dangerous, believing their thoughts and/or hallucinations are real and when no one else believes them, become antagonistic and defensive. When families seek help for an individual manifesting such symptoms, the journey to wellness can begin, although it may be a long and arduous journey.

The current thought is that schizophrenia is caused by a myriad of factors: genetic, environmental, or chemical. The brains of a schizophrenic simply looks different than one of a normal individual.

Hum, think about it….In Biblical times, people saw God. They talked to God. And God talked to them. Those visitations were considered miracles. What would we call them today in our Western culture?

I'm seriously not trying to bash religion or question those events chronicled as miracles, but merely pointing out that "different strokes for different folks" is definitely a good descriptor.

Psychology is a social science – not a pure science, but psychologists and other psychobabble stewards try their hardest to make it a science. That's why we have a DSM-5 today. We can diagnose symptoms just like medical doctors.

The simple truth is that all medicine is subjective in the end. Sometimes doctors get it right and sometimes they simply don't. It is the same way with psychobabble people – sometimes we are right on in our diagnosis of a mental condition and sometimes we are far off in left field. Could it be that sometimes God **IS** talking to us?

As I mentioned before, one of the best films I have ever viewed is *A Beautiful Mind.* I watched it twice and the second time with my husband and son. I made the mistake of giving away the premise too soon and they still haven't forgiven me for that! I still feel so guilty that I have repeated that fact twice in this book….

But as you watch the movie, you really do get in the mind of a person diagnosed with schizophrenia. The movie is based on the life of John Nash, a Nobel Prize awardee (he was **really** smart and won lots of recognition and honor for his study in economics).

He was an eccentric individual who displayed enormous intelligence in the field of mathematics and generally was not liked by most of his peers, but admired for his intelligence alone. He did not develop his mental illness until he was into his 30s.

His life became a whirl of brilliance and decadence – being committed twice involuntarily to a mental institution.

Surprisingly, when he got older, Nash recovered enough from this disease to remarry his wife, regain his family, and return to work as a research professor.

Somehow individuals diagnosed with schizophrenia can recover from their illness sufficiently so to enjoy what seems to be a normal lifestyle. That is the good news.

The bad news is that many individuals do not receive adequate treatment for their illness and these same individuals endure life with pain and agony.

Stress seemed to be the trigger for Nash as it is for many diagnosed with schizophrenia. The important thing to remember is that there is hope for those afflicted with this anomaly and the best way with which to deal with it is to consult with the professionals in the mental health industry.

Think of someone in your life who talks about visions – seeing or hearing what God tells them to do. Is this person mentally ill or religious? Why do you think so?

Chapter 10

Is there hope?

Never give up on someone with a mental illness. When "I" is replaced by "We", illness becomes wellness."

Shannon L. Alder

As stated in the last chapter, individuals are able to recover from diagnoses from mental illnesses, even from schizophrenia. And as I also said, our Western culture deems some acts illnesses that were formerly, in other times, considered miraculous behaviors and even simply gifted events.

The treatment of disease/illness is predicated upon the mores of the times. In this day and age, we look to give equal rights to those who practice homosexuality. In the 60s these individuals' behavior was deemed abnormal.

In some cultures it is quite acceptable and, indeed the norm, to demonstrate high levels of emotional drama in every aspect of one's life. In our Western culture, these individuals are slapped with labels such as borderline personality disorder, narcissism, or some other nomenclature.

So how do you know when to seek professional help for yourself or for another individual? The rule of thumb simply is that if the behavior causes a noticeable and unusual disruption of the

individual's life, those symptoms need to be assessed by a qualified professional.

Many ways exist to help people become well-adjusted, happier, or simply less stressed.

Who can help with these problems? An array of professionals and quasi-professionals await you and it might behoove you to know the differences between them.

A psychiatrist is a medical doctor. S/he is primarily a doctor and in our culture that means s/he is trained to diagnose, prescribe, and treat. Medication. This individual is most apt to give you medicine if they think you need it – and maybe even if you don't.

A session with a psychiatrist usually does not entail long-winded conversations. No, the doctor will ask you questions, type your responses, and give you some meds and tell you to come back in a week or a month….

Psychologists are individuals with a doctorate in psychology. They are trained in a variety of venues,

but will not be dispensing medication – that's the MD's role.

The Ph.D. in psychology will listen, converse, and ask questions and, hopefully, work in tandem with your physician to deliver the most useful treatment.

A counselor (depending on the state) may have a variety of advanced degrees, including a master's in social work, an art therapy counseling master's, or a counseling master's.

These counselors are trained also in a variety of methods, but most are familiar with methodologies that help you reframe your thinking process – so if you are easily hurt or upset about things, they can teach you how to not be so. Seriously, they can! I only wish I had learned some of these things before I was a senior citizen. It would have helped me tremendously in my early career and social life as well. I'm still not sure why I didn't learn these things, but being from a different culture is probably one of the contributing factors.

Each of us basically wants to be happy and what that entails for each of us differs vastly. When our behavior gets in the way of that happiness and fulfillment, then we begin to see a problem emerging.

It's best to nip it in the bud, so to speak. Don't wait until the symptoms are so engrained in you that they are difficult to remove.

For instance, if you have a child who is constantly angry – you simply must start examining the cause of that anger and try to help the child see alternative ways to deal with stress rather than acting out with anger.

The same goes for teens and adults. Mental illness can come upon one at any stage of life and family and close friends are our moral support systems that will and should help us through hard times.

The key is to realize when there is a problem. Sometimes we don't see the problem ourselves and it is our significant others who see it. That's when we need them to help us either see it for ourselves or ensure that we are seen by a professional to establish a base line and improvement plan.

Yes, there is hope. There is only no hope when you stick your head in the sand and pretend there is no problem. There is no hope when you refuse to listen to others and think you have all the answers.

Mankind is a social race. We need others. Some of us need fewer humans around us than others, but we all need friends and loved ones who will be there for us when we need them – in good times and in bad.

Write down five names of people you consider your moral support system. Draw them or write their names down. Let them know they are important to you by writing to them or giving them a call! Keep them in the loop with your life.

Chapter 11

Humor

"But Hey, Guess What
Crazy means I'm not liable
for my actions. So screw it,
I'll go home, propped up on
Prozac against distractions."

Ellen Hopkins, Impulse

Recently, Robin Williams committed suicide in a horrific manner. So why am I starting out a chapter on humor mentioning this dark act?

Simply because I loved the movie in which Mr. Williams played a doctor who believed in humor in healing. The movie to which I refer was "Patch Adams."

The real Patch Adams is involved in radical medicine, in that he wants to make sure everyone receives adequate treatment. He has a website http://patchadams.org/mission that tells about his mission, a nonprofit in the District of Columbia, which is a project in holistic medical care. Their premise is that one cannot separate the health of the individual from the health of the family, the community, the world, and the health care system itself.

Read and believe!

- Medical care is free.
- Patients are treated as friends.
- Complementary medicine is welcome.

- Health of staff is as important as health of patients.
- Care is infused with fun and play.

For sure, being treated by a clown would be a novel idea! Adams is a clown as well as physician, healer, and entrepreneur. If every person who reads these words took one day to do something nice for another human being, this could become such a better and more healing world.

Japanese geneticist Dr. Kazuo Murakami, one of the top geneticists in the world and Professor Emeritus at the University of Tsukuba, Japan, states that "laughter is a stimulant, which can trigger energy inside a person's DNA potentially helping cure disease. A laughing therapy has no side-effect, meaning it is an epoch-making treatment for clinical medicine. If we prove people can switch genes on and off by an emotion like laughter, it may be the finding of the century which should be worth the Nobel Prize or even go beyond that."

In Laughter Yoga, the premise is that laughing out loud is healthy and the individual does not have to have a reason to laugh – he or she simply laughs out loud! There is more to it, so if you are interested, check out this website:

http://2014.laughteryogaamerica.com/

Books exist that talk about the benefits of humor in a medical setting. Hum, let's see, the colonoscopy – everyone will eventually (well, everyone should, they say) get one! And if you don't have a sense of humor, this can be a dark few days for you!

But as I got to the hospital for the dreaded IV (the worst thing about the whole procedure as far as I was concerned), the nurses talked with me and laughed around, joking, putting me at ease. Yeah, the needle still hurt and I was still apprehensive, but feeling much better while laughing. And then the rest is history and I don't remember a thing until I woke up.

Who doesn't like looking at animal antics and laughing? Such innocent little videos can create a sense of well-being.

You've probably heard the advice given to those who are afraid to get up in front of others to speak. They are told to "imagine the crowd sitting there without any clothes on," or when the boss yells at you (or someone else for that matter), "think of holes in their head and steam coming out." Those little visualizations help us deal with life in a calmer and healthier fashion.

Humor does not have to be a laugh out loud situation. Wellness and being joyous can be partners. Several websites are dedicated to creating joyous patients AND professional staff.

When I was a bored high school student, I created diversions to enable me to endure the days. One was looking at the social studies book and writing (no, I don't THINK I wrote in books, but, hey, maybe I did….) captions that were funny to me for photographs in the texts.

I would share these with a classmate or two and we would generally experience a communal guffaw.

Then a few friends and I created a club making fun of ourselves – called the Cow Club. Most of us were tall for that era – and most of the boys were shorter than we were, so calling each other cows seemed funny at the time.

Today I look back and shake my head at the silliness of it all, but since I remember it, it must have had some effect on me and I can still laugh a bit at how silly we innocent girls were.

When we would pass one another in the hall, we would moo. Is that silly or what? Maybe crazy!

One girl in the club and I recently met after 45 years and both remembered the Cow Club. Ah, the innocence of youth. It helped smooth the passage of bored young women through a mandatory stage in their lives.

I have frequently advised my students and children to laugh inside when they are angry at someone – to think of something funny and to smile.

Smiling, even though we are crying on the inside, can actually activate pheromones that will make us feel better. What a miracle our body is!

The essence of holistic healing is to utilize all these methodologies to create a healthier lifestyle. So smile more often! Laugh and find people and events that make you happy. It's contagious, you know.

Laughing can be healing. Watch a truly funny sitcom or movie and after laughing out loud, notice how much better you feel? Draw how you feel.

Chapter 12

DSM 5 Therapy Bible

Published by the American Psychiatric Association, it is, in the APA's words, the *standard classification of mental disorders used by mental health professionals in the United States. It is intended to be applicable in a wide array of contexts and used by clinicians and researchers of many different orientations. . . It can be used by a wide range of health and mental health professionals, including psychiatrists and other physicians, psychologists, social workers, nurses, occupational and rehabilitation therapists, and counselors.*

It is commonly referred to as the 'mental health Bible.'

In counseling school it became evident to me that I had many more mental illnesses than I formerly suspected. Yes, the medical student syndrome was alive and well in a few of us as we perused the many-paged reference book for mental illnesses.

I furtively asked a classmate if she thought I might be borderline personality; she looked at me and shook her head, "No, Lola, definitely not." Then I looked at her and wondered at her diagnostic skills....

The DSM 5, the fifth edition of the Diagnostic Statistical Manual of Mental Disorders, is used widely in the United States. All mental health practitioners are familiar with this text and most use it to bill insurance, which is the first clue you might imagine – it is about money and billing.

Many psycho-babble folks do not believe the current edition is correct, useful, and/or comprehensive. In the 1840s the census carried a characteristic – insane/idiocy, and the rest is history. We need to categorize and label. It is just what we do. Our country continued to need a label for maladies, mostly for returning soldiers after World

War I. The American Psychiatric Association was born out of such a need and the beginnings of a need for a code and comprehensive book of mental disorders was begun.

After World War II, the World Health Organization (WHO) published the sixth edition of *International Classification of Diseases (*ICD), which, for the first time, included a section for mental disorders. ICD-6 was heavily influenced by the Veterans Administration nomenclature and included 10 categories for psychoses and psychoneuroses and seven categories for disorders of character, behavior, and intelligence.

The birth of the first DSM was in 1952. It was widely embraced by the medical community – we psychotherapists were just like medical doctors – we had diseases we could diagnose and categorize and then we could bill insurance as well.

The DSM 5 is almost 1,000 pages of probably 8 font words describing behavior from bed wetting to full blown psychosis. Therapists are trained in the use of the DSM and learn how to diagnose through various classes and   practice sessions.

I was lucky to have a wonderful partner in counseling school where we would alternate times "counseling" one another as we were videotaped and later able to view and discuss our particular styles. To counsel and then to receive a critique on our effectiveness was a mind opening experience.

Back to the DSM-5....Each disorder starts with a descriptive summary of what the illness is. Each is assigned a number IF the diagnostic criteria are met. A handy list of criteria is displayed in a checklist format.

Next come some associated features and development and the course of the disease, as well as risk and prognostic features. Even some cultural consideration is given to the therapist to consider and then a brief section on comorbidity is put forth.

Ever wonder why therapists charge so much money? For one, at least two years of fulltime study are required for a Master's level degree, but more for a doctorate, and even more for medical school. You get the picture – high tuition cost. This, of course, is in addition to the undergraduate degree which takes at least four   years to complete.

Each professional must also have insurance, so that they *do no harm* and if they do, they are insured so when sued, they don't lose their home, car, and kids.

Also, just graduating from a counseling program is not enough, even though the practitioner does an internship and takes numerous tests – each state is different but in Oregon one must have at least 1000 more supervised hours and then take another test in order to qualify for a LPC (Licensed Professional Counselor). This supervisor must be paid an hourly fee ranging from $100 and up.

Books also come at quite a cost. Proficient and caring therapists will continually update their skills and read the latest in counseling literature, oftentimes joining professional organizations, at a cost that needs to be recouped.

And then we have the office where the professional wants you to be relaxed and comfortable. Furnishings can add up to a substantial cost.

Tie it all together and the therapist needs to charge at least $100 an hour, since he or she must use the other unpaid times to write notes, read literature, discuss cases with the supervisor, and bill clients.

There is even more, but now, perhaps, the average citizen can understand why the cost of therapy is not small. Good therapy can make the difference between a good life and a joyous one.

Look in the phone book (do they exist anymore?) and see how many mental health therapists there are. What are some of the other descriptors of these individuals? How many have offices near where you live?

Chapter 13

Art Therapy

"The task of therapy is not to eliminate suffering but to give a voice to it, to find a form in which it can be expressed. Expression is itself transformation; this is the message that art brings. The therapist then would be an artist of the soul, working with sufferers to enable them to find the proper container for their pain, the form in which it would be embodied."

Stephen K. Levine

How did it all start? How did I even find out about art therapy, as I am not an accomplished artist, nor did I ever take an art class before going to graduate school? My own mother was aghast that I was going to get a second master's in ART THERAPY!

We don't do art. Our family just doesn't. Why?

I won her over by asking her to draw something, to which she replied in a huff, *You know I don't draw.* And I simply told her to scribble. And, boy, did she! She gripped the pencil so hard I thought she might break it. As she began to draw concentric circles with such energy, I began laughing.

When she was finished, she asked me what I could say about her! Well, if I did not know this lady for a very long time, I still would have been able to ascertain that she was filled with tremendous energy, you know, kind of like the energizer bunny? I also know that it was very evident that once she begins a task, she is unlikely to complete it very soon.

She was amazed and finally relented, *I get it now. I see what you are talking about. That is really helpful.*

Before becoming an art therapist, I had never heard of the field nor had I any illusions of becoming a counselor. But one thing I knew, according to my adult students, is that my class was like therapy. The only thing I did differently than other teachers, I concede, is that I used a **lot** of the expressive arts – movement, art, music, and drama. And people enjoyed the time in my class.

I looked online and was fortunate to find a program less than an hour away from my home and I enrolled, albeit it was not that easy – I had never taken an art class as I said before, so I had to take a year of art classes. I loved learning how to draw – learned that everyone can learn to draw. I took at least nine semester hours in painting, drawing, and sculpture each. By the end of the art classes, I realized I loved sculpture the best. Art takes on many forms, so with art therapy it depends on what works for the client. It is the job of the therapist to figure this out.

When working with Alzheimer's clients, I used simple media to ensure success. Each one had a wonderful time and each individual created a totally different project. They were happy and relaxed and calm, which is a great goal to have for an Alzheimer

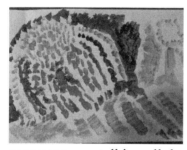 client. This one perseverated about colors and loved working with dabbling.

An older gentleman loved making separate trees, talking all the while about trees of different seasons. His painting pleased him and his family as well.

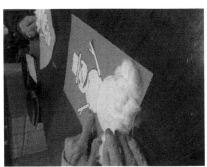

One client enjoyed putting together a snowman. When her table mates were finished as well, we put them on the wall and talked about how different they all were, even though each had the same kind of materials. Great conversation for any group.

119

I like to say that art therapy is like talk therapy PLUS. The plus can be illustrated in an example of a young boy who came into my office last year. He was angrier than any little kid I had ever seen. He was throwing this wacky wall sticky thing. For a moment I thought he might toss it at me. He didn't. After a few minutes, I looked at him and said, "Boy, you sure are mad today!"

Duh! He looked at me as if I had three eyes. *You are darn right! I'm madder than that!*

To which I suggested he sit down and show me with colors how mad he really was. He drew a head and colored in with great fury with red, then blue, and with a more relaxed stance, used the green crayon.

I asked him to tell me about his picture. He said the following

Everyone knows red means you are mad. I am mad a lot. And the blue means I am sad. I am sad a lot, too. And, well, the green, is happy, and I'm not happy much.

I agreed that he felt those things and suggested that he think about things that made him happy.

Riding my bike.

So he ended up drawing a bike and with a cut and paste moment covered up some of the red. We talked about not replacing angry feelings, but making choices to not be so angry all the time. He got the idea and before you know it, he had taken

the time to find a lot of things he liked doing and his head appeared a bit happier. I don't think we could have accomplished this problem solving in such a short time just by talking. The art allows the client to activate more quickly and to allow the individual to make better connections.

The child realized that having feelings are normal – it's just how we act on them that is important. He left my office smiling and a little happier. Of course, we still needed to work on his anger issues more, but that was a good start.

Another child had extreme separation anxiety from her mom (I suspected Mom had more issues as well). The little girl was very serious and so I tried a bit of humor with her and her friend who came to visit me once a week. We told developmentally appropriate jokes and after a month I finally saw this child smile and then laugh out loud. She began to relax.

She drew things that made her laugh. The two little girls in my office guffawing over something few would find funny was intensely gratifying to me. She loved coming to see me and I know why – she was relaxed and happy – something I hoped would transfer to the classroom.

Her last visit she asked me if she could take her funny pictures with her. Who knew snakes could be so funny?

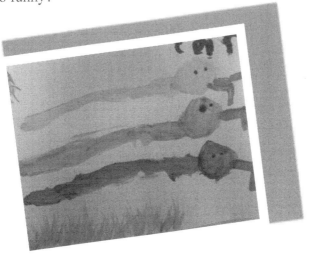

The field of art therapy is rife with conflict. Some say it is psychotherapy (well, I was trained in psychotherapy in my art therapy program – weren't we all? I suspect not….). Others say it is counseling, and yet others state it is quite different than either of those. Even the credentialing boards disagree. In Oregon, a credentialed art therapist cannot bill insurance, but a credentialed counselor may. It is quite obvious which credential is more important to me – I want to provide services to underprivileged individuals and in so doing, must be able to get partial reimbursement from insurance.

A difference also exists in saying art therapy and art AS therapy. I have seen individuals claim they are art therapists when they do not have a master's degree in art therapy. They might have taken a class or two or read about using art and, in so doing, are using art AS therapy. These folks are NOT art therapists.

Making any kind of art is therapeutic, that is true. I even wrote a book about using art to work out retirement issues. This workbook explains that it is using art as therapy and that reading the book does not mean one has experienced art therapy. In art therapy, a trained art therapy counselor knows all about the developmental stages of art, the nuances, the directives, and the way to discuss the art in a positive fashion with the client.

Art therapists do not interpret client art. They simply ask questions to help the client think about things not articulated previously. For instance, when a young girl drew a tree before, during, and after a storm, I asked her to tell me about the tree and the storm. She admitted that the tree sort of enjoyed the storm and was strong afterwards, only having lost a few leaves.

When I asked her to tell me about her life, she (and this is a nine year old) began to tell me about storms with her siblings. She says she stays strong like the tree by reading in solitude in her bedroom.

We had lots to talk about, but the art facilitated the words for this child. She began to see that she is in charge of how she feels and how she acts, regardless of her siblings' actions.

People do not have to "like" art to enjoy doing art therapy. I have a very good friend who says she does not *think* she would enjoy doing art therapy. How does she know if she has not tried it? I suspect she thinks it is just making beautiful art. Sometimes the art my clients make is not beautiful. Anything but. It is not the kind of art we would show to others to admire. Quite possibly we would share it with other counselors who would want to learn about the process, but never, never would I have an art show of my clients' work. All that stuff about privacy, client privilege, etc….No, those pieces of art belong to the client and I always allow my client to take his or her art home. I take a digital photo of it and file it with the rest of the client's information.

I encourage students when I am in the classroom to doodle and I highly encourage the teachers to allow that. I am the type of person who likes to doodle (and it is not beautiful art, I assure you) while listening to a lecture or, sometimes even while watching a television show. It helps me focus and relax. It seems to do the same sort of thing for others as well….

Look up mandalas. What are they? Print one out and color it or create your own below.

Chapter 14

Meds

...Some of us care for orphans, amass fortunes, raise protests or Nielsen ratings; some of us take communion or whiskey or poison. Some of us take lithium and antidepressants, and most everyone believes these pills are fundamentally wrong, a crutch, a sign of moral weakness, the surrender of art and individuality...Without medicine, 20 percent of us, one in five, will commit suicide. Six-gun Russian roulette gives better odds. Denouncing these medicines makes as much sense as denouncing the immorality of motor oil. Without them, sooner or later the bipolar brain will go bang. I know plenty of potheads who sermonize against the pharmaceutical companies; I know plenty of born-again yoga instructors, plenty of missionaries who tell me I'm wrong about lithium. They don't have a clue."

David Lovelace, *Scattershot: My Bipolar Family*

The Food and Drug Administration (FDA) has a website that is sure to boggle your mind. Checking it out, I found hundreds of recalled pharmaceutical products, from pills guaranteed to enhance male virility to catheters used in the home. And I wondered. I wondered how many of the average folk (even the above average folk, to be honest) ever even check out this site. Who advertises this site? Who encourages the consumer-client-patient-individual to check it out and seek the state of their medication's safety?

Most of us, I suspect, rely on the provider's knowledge of medication safety. If our doctor prescribes it, it has to be good. If our pharmacist dispenses it, it must be good. And we go on our merry way....

I know one young man who takes a cocktail of medications to keep him stable and productive. But is he stable and productive? His inner demons are constantly battling him and when he shares this with his psychiatrist, another pill is added to the regimen. Rarely is one taken off. His parents are worried and questioning the medical personnel's investment into this young man's life. This young man is a shell of what he used to be. Is this necessary or is it time for others to advocate for him, causing an intensive review of all the medications and therapies used up to now?

Sometimes meds are necessary for life and balance. Sometimes not. How does one know the difference?

According to Web MD, some of the most commonly used medications for treating mental illnesses are antidepressants, anti-anxiety, anti-psychotic, mood stabilizing, and stimulant medications.

And how does a doctor determine which medication is right for each patient? Is it error proof? Or is it an educated guess?

Centuries ago, before the advent of antibiotics, people died of bacterial infections. Today we are blessed with antibiotics that can cure those same infections, yet administered too freely, these same antibiotics are rendered ineffectual by some resistant strains of bacteria.

It's true to say that medication is to an extent an inexact science. We do pretty well considering those who came before us, but some day there will be better and newer ways to treat mental illnesses. As they say in the commercial, we have come a long way, baby.

Some mental illnesses can be controlled or perhaps even eradicated with therapy. Some need meds + therapy. Rarely is it advised that someone just receive meds and no therapy.

The menu that is most effectual according to recent research is the combination of medication and therapy. People taking medication need to realize that they need to establish an open and communicative relationship with their medical servers. Reporting side effects truthfully and completely will help the provider to diagnose and prescribe more appropriate medication and treatment.

Sometimes people just get tired of the meds and stop them cold turkey. All medical professionals agree that patients should check first with their doctor before stopping meds. And, if one is to stop a med, it is best done gradually, so as to not upset the delicate balance in one's system.

Some meds need to be taken with water and others on empty stomachs. Some need to be taken in the morning and some in the evening. It is the duty of the patient or his/her family to be aware of the particular nuances of each medication. If you don't know, then ask questions. The local pharmacist is a great source of information regarding medication.

What about alternative medications, those not regulated by the FDA? Are they safe or are we again at the mercy of large companies? Lately, large essential oil companies have touted their oils (either ingested or used topically) as panaceas for all sorts of ill – smelling lavender or peppermint can elevate your mood….

"I'm not aware of any evidence essential oils can influence the course of any disease," says Dr. Stephen Barrett, a retired psychiatrist who runs quackwatch.org and is critical of alternative medicine claims.

Dr. David Gorsky, who writes a column online at sciencebasedmedicine.org, says there is no alleged documented evidence to prove the claims of essential oil companies.

To be fair, the large essential oil companies rely on testimonies and anecdotes to tout their efficacy. In the long run, they aren't scientifically researched adequately, according to most physicians. They can have a placebo effect and everyone can agree that a whiff of peppermint can indeed energize one temporarily.

It is evident that more study and research needs to be completed, so buyer beware. Do your research and try sparingly at first. If it works for you, who cares if it is a placebo effect or actually the oil that helps? Baby steps, baby steps....

If a mixture of peppermint oil soothes your stomach, who is to say that is not alright? Who is to say that diffusing lavender at night isn't a good way to calm yourself? The point most doctors are making is that unless it has been proven, we are not sure that certain meds or oils or procedures will work most of the time. That does not mean they don't. It also doesn't mean they won't. Essential oils are different in that they are more potent and less is needed to use of them, and, hopefully, most are pure oil, with no additives, which makes them appeal to the purifists among us. (Yes, I think that is a made up word, but I like it, don't you?)

Many medications can have disturbing side effects. It then becomes necessary to balance the good the meds do against the negative. The patient must work with a team – the prescribing physician, therapist, pharmacist—all working to creating a more harmonious and joyous life for the patient/client.

We are currently learning things about drugs that were not formerly known. For instance, in the 50's women were given Thalidomide to calm nausea and many deformed babies were born as a result. The medication crossed the placenta wall and infected the forming child.

Another anti-nausea drug called Bendectin was also freely prescribed in the 70's and many resulting birth defects were attributed to the combination of an antihistamine and B6. Today both drugs are banned in the United States. Are these drugs truly to be blamed for birth defects? Apparently there is a chance they are. Is that chance worth taking?

When certain antidepressants seemed to create suicidal behavior in children and teens, the FDA posted a warning on such medications so the general public could be aware of the dire consequences of taking such a pill. What is the result? The FDA and health professionals say that these meds can be helpful to children and teens, but these same individuals must be closely monitored. Again, is it worth the chance?

One point is worth being stressed over and over again – buyer beware! Health professionals, particularly physicians, are not gods. I was raised to believe they knew what was right and it was not proper to question their directives. I now know better. Educate yourself. There is no excuse with the plethora of information available online to not know the pros and cons of medication prescribed to you and your loved one.

Making choices can be difficult. When one of our sons was a toddler, he walked with his feet pointing outward. One physician advised us to do surgery which would mean he would be in a body cast for more than four months. The physician also said there would be a 40% chance of making his life better.

After checking with our pediatrician, we decided against the surgery. Today he is a healthy young man, very adept at running, and only vestiges of his former disability appear occasionally. It was a choice we made after a lot of deliberation. Choices are difficult.

Go to the internet and find the site below. Find out what your pills should look like. Why are they different and why should you care?

http://www.webmd.com/pill-identification/default.htm

Chapter 15

Holistic Healing

"I shall be telling this with a sigh
Somewhere ages and ages hence:
Two roads diverged in a wood, and I --
I took the one less traveled by,
And that has made all the difference."

Robert Frost, The Road Not Taken

We are all guilty of jumping on the bandwagon to better our lifestyle. Diets, pills, panaceas for a joyous and healthy life….The sad fact is that many folks in our culture today learn their facts (or so they deem them) from social media, be it the internet or television or radio. So if they have a headache, a small white round pill might do the trick. You can even get pills to keep an erection up longer….this, my friends, advertised on prime time TV.

But, wait! Perhaps a look at one's diet would be more informative. When do you get those headaches? Frequently? Occasionally? What have you eaten before? Have you had enough sleep? Are you having a spat with someone? All these questions serve to help the WHOLE individual, hence holistic healing.

I know that my knees hurt like crazy when I go up and down stairs when I have not been exercising regularly. If I took an aspirin or ibuprofen or Tylenol each time they hurt, I'd be hooked on meds. Or I would simply need more and more each time to get the same effect.

Holistic healing involves not only traditional medicine, but alternative healing strategies as well. Once I read in a group that yoga was not allowed in a certain Christian religion. Are you kidding me? It's an exercise program in this day and age. Yes, it is associated with many other cultural aspects, but I highly doubt any group in this country practicing yoga are consciously practicing religious practices.

The few times I did pilates (an off shoot of yoga), I remarked that I had NEVER and I do mean, never, felt that great before. I felt a sensation of loving how I felt. That has to be good stuff, folks.

Do we take the easy road or the difficult road? Do we take the road most others take or do we choose the road according to what is best for us?

When I was younger and raising my children I simply did what I could. Not more. I had a career, an education to pursue, and three little boys to raise. Hubby was a wonderful father, but the household chores were my domain, hence the reason my children will always have a tender spot in their hearts for McDonald's.

I cringe now that I may have helped them make poor choices for their nutritional needs. One thing I have learned is that we cannot undo what happened in the past and before I beat myself up with guilt, I just remember I loved my family and did the best I could at the time.

Exercise is extremely important in mental health. Walking and talking can cure many a depressive or anxious mood. Dancing, music, and art - all these provide a healing hormone to the body. These alternative therapies are not superfluous, they are necessary to our joy as humans.

Massage therapy is one of those alternative therapies that most people feel guilty about, but shouldn't. The massage therapist who can eradicate pain from your body and/or connect with your stress and lower it is a healer by all rights.

Several studies have been done on individuals who began regular exercise and the majority of those individuals reported fewer colds and aches and pains as a result.

Acupuncture is a procedure many people swear by and may be something to try in the event traditional medicine is not doing the trick. Some people even try it as their first choice.

http://nccam.nih.gov/

The above referenced web address explains more about alternative therapies, including chiropractic care. We are so lucky in this day and age to be able to obtain a multitude of curative therapies for our ills – all we need to do is research them and educate ourselves about what might be best for each of us.

Being an informed consumer helps you make the best decisions at the time for you and your loved ones. Realizing that not all therapies are the right fit for each individual, you should take the time to make decisions about all your medical care by finding out what scientific studies have been done on the effectiveness and/or safety of a product or practice of interest to you.

By checking out this web address you can find resources to help you make informed decisions about issues and questions to ask as well.

It is up to you to locate alternative therapists, but always check their credentials, education, training, and licensure. Ask whether they have treated someone with similar symptoms as you. Discuss the pay method and don't assume insurance will cover your choice of treatment.

One of the best things you can do is to be communicative and tell all your doctors, therapists, and health care providers about all practitioners working with you. In that vein, each one will be able to be part of a team that works uniquely with you. Being a responsible, assertive client or patient will bring you the most satisfaction in obtaining the best healthcare for you.

It's about this time that I begin to prepare my clients for closure with me. We still have a little way to go but our journey together will soon end. In the same vein, with you, dear reader, I want you to know that we have both learned some skills with which to make our lives better. Take those skills and practice them. Share them with others and, more importantly, take good care of your mind, your body, and your soul. You are the only one who can do so and the choice to a healthy and productive life is yours. Choose wisely!

Certainly most of us have heard the "be in the moment" admonition. It makes sense – we can't change the past nor live in the future, but we can certainly be in the present. Being in the present doesn't mean we don't remember nor does it mean we can't plan for the future. It means that we need so spend more time in the present. That old 'smell the roses' advice. It works. We will never have another minute like right now.

One year I was teaching 8th graders and they were getting kind of testy and talking and not listening and all that other prepubescence stuff. So I told them to be quiet for just one minute. We would watch the second hand on the clock. They complied (to my great surprise). Afterwards I told them that they had just spent one minute of their life that they would never get back. So they needed to take time to enjoy each minute of their life and not waste it. Of course, one smart-alec asked me why I was wasting their time! But they did get the message.

Moving in any way you are able also helps with improving your mental health. You have heard the 'use it or lose it' slogan, right? Well, it simply means that if we don't move and exercise, our bodies will begin to deteriorate. What happens when our body deteriorates? We feel badly and then our mind is made up that negativity reigns supreme in our lives. The rest is history. Yes, movement is great for mental and physical health.

Dancing, yoga, exercise classes, walking, jogging, running, swimming or just walking in the water – find something you like to do and you will more than likely do it more than once. I can already feel the warm water at the Courthouse Athletic Club where I've been a member for years. I can't swim but I certainly can play in the water, walking from side to side, jumping up and down and being just silly. But any movement works, I promise you!

And, last, but certainly not least, is the power of prayer. Studies have shown that individuals who pray and believe in God actually weather stress and illnesses better.

According to WebMD, even distant praying helps those in need! What exactly is this distant praying, you ask? Certainly you have heard of prayer chains within groups and churches. That's what distant praying can be. It can also be that I ask all my family to pray for you as you face something difficult in your life. How exactly does this work?

WebMD goes on to explain that in the last ten years (we are in the year 2014), praying healing has doubled in this country. Is there something to this universe – a god, if you will, who will help us when asked. Some people think so.

Are we wired for spirituality? Harvard scientist H. Benson, MD, conducted studies on prayer, specifically meditation. You will recognize that as a form of Buddhist prayer. He wanted to see exactly how our mind affects our body. He reports that any kind of prayer can evoke a healing for it can help quieten the body and forestall stress.

His definition of prayer is "repetition—of sounds, words, and therein lies its healing effects." Admitting that every religion has a different way of praying, he has documented MRI brain sans the actual physical changes that takes place in the body during meditation. Here's what he has found:

As an individual goes deeper and deeper into concentration, intense activity begins taking place in the brain's parietal lobe circuits -- those that control a person's orientation in space and establish distinctions between self and the world. Benson has documented a "quietude" that then envelops the entire brain.

At the same time, frontal and temporal lobe circuits -- which track time and create self-awareness -- become disengaged. The mind-body connection dissolves, Benson says.

And the limbic system, which is responsible for putting "emotional tags" on that which we consider special, also becomes activated. The limbic system also regulates relaxation, ultimately controlling the autonomic nervous system, heart rate, blood pressure, metabolism, etc.

The exciting result is that all systems register a sense of awe and quiet as the body becomes more relaxed and all physiological activity regulation becomes even

Although science can document these changes and effects, it cannot affirm the existence of God – that is up to the religious to do. It is called *faith.*

I have faith in you, dear reader!

Schedule a massage for yourself. Join a gym. Walk in the park. Take up a new hobby. Take photographs of all the beautiful nature in your community. Take a deep breath. Breathe through your nose deeply and exhale slowly. Close your eyes. Be thankful you are alive. Smile. Live!

Write three new things you will try to enhance your total health. Draw you in that new mode. Ahhh....

Fare thee well...

And so now we've just ended our journey together and I am saddened – mainly because I haven't gotten to know you and that's what is important. If this book helps you in a small way, I have served my purpose. What are your secrets to living a healthy and purposeful life?

I'd love to hear from you – email me at masabitherapist@gmail.com and let me know what is working in your life. May we all make this journey we call life purposeful and joyous together.

Peace and blessings,

Lola

Bibliography

American Psychiatric Association. (2013). *Diagnostic and statistical manual of mental disorders* (5th ed.). Washington, DC: Author.

Baumann, B., Bielau, H. and Bernstein, H.-G. (2002). *A depression neurocircuit. Evidence from structural and functional studies.* Bipolar Disorders, 4: 85.

Grazer, B., Howard, R., Goldsman, A., Crowe, R., Harris, E., Connelly, J., Bettany, P. Imagine Entertainment (Firm). (2002). *A beautiful mind.* Willowdale, Ont: Distributed by Universal Studios Canada.

http://nccam.nih.gov/

http://www.autismspeaks.org/what-autism/diagnosis/screen-your-child

http://www.coloring-pages-for-all-ages.com/adult-coloring-pages.html

151

http://www.fda.gov/

http://www.mayoclinic.org/diseases-
conditions/depression/basics/definition/con-
20032977

http://www.mayoclinic.org/search/search-
results?q=personality%20disorders

http://www.medscape.com/viewarticle/529308

http://www.merriam-webster.com/

http://www.patchadams.org/

http://www.sciencebasedmedicine.org/

http://www.webmd.com/balance/features/can-
prayer-heal

http://www.buddhanet.net/mandalas.htm

Murakami, Kazuo (2006). *The Divine Code of Life.*
New York: Atria Books/Beyond Words.

Patch Adams [Motion picture]. (1999). Universal.

Pilot. *The Big Bang Theory*. CBS. WYOU, Scranton. 27
Sept. 2007. Television.

Sadeghi, Habib (2013). *Within: A Spiritual
Awakening to Love & Weight Loss.* Los
Angeles, CA: Premier Digital Publishing.

Recommended Reading

B. Ssemakula, Fr. Yozefu. (2011). *The Healing of Families.* Keizer, OR: WalkingWord, Inc.

Carnegie, Dale. (1981). *How to Win Friends and Influence Enemies.* New York: Simon and Schuster.

Detrich, R.L., Steele, Nicola. (1996). *How to Recover from Grief.* New York: Judson Publishing Co.

Fonseca, Christine. (2011). *Emotional Intensity in Gifted Students.* Waco, TX: Prufrock Inc.

Honore, Carl. (2005). *In Praise of Slowness.* New York: Orion Publishing Co.

Isay, Jane. (2007). *Walking on Eggshells.* New York: Anchor Books, Inc.

Kranowitz, Carol Stock. (2005). *The Out of Sync Child.* New York: Berkeley Press.

Littauer, Florence. (1992). *Personality Plus.* Grand
    Rapids, MI: Baker Book House Co.

O'Connor, Richard. (2010). *Undoing Depression.*
    New York: Little, Brown, & Co.

Peter, Dan. (2013). *Make Your Worrier a Warrior*.
    Tucson, AZ: Great Potential Press.

Peters, Dan. (2013). *From Worrier to Warrior.*
    Tucson, AZ: Great Potential Press.

Sadeghi, Habib. (2014). *Within: A Spiritual
    Awakening to Love & Weight Loss.*

Appendix I

Following are some ideas for creating art that both relaxes and helps one focus better.

Art as Therapy Disclaimer

Try any of the following art experiences to promote a sense of peace and tranquility as well as a time to learn to focus better! Remember that art therapy occurs when a trained art therapist (one usually with a Master's or better in art therapy counseling) works with you as you produce your art. Just doing art **IS** therapeutic and helpful. Sometimes counselors and physicians not trained in art therapy counseling will use art in their sessions with clients. They are not doing art therapy just as I am not doing music therapy when I play some soft music in my sessions. With that said, the reason I am making this perfectly clear to you is that sometimes certain kinds of art can evoke feelings and emotions that a trained art therapist will know requires careful use of materials. Some materials actually create a digression scenario for the client which can become dicey, if not actually dangerous.

Yin and Yang

In ancient China a philosophy emerged that talked about a person's being. As whole beings, we all have good and bad within us, hence the symbol of yin and yang: good and evil. When balanced, the whole is unperturbed. When unbalanced, chaos, craziness, and other mayhem rules....

 Either draw a large circle and fill in or draw "positive" things about you and then to be fair, draw in "negative" things about you. Use different colors to differentiate. Determine if you are in balance and take a moment to figure out which "negative" element you wish to work on....the next page is yours to draw, write, etc. Enjoy.

Yin and Yang

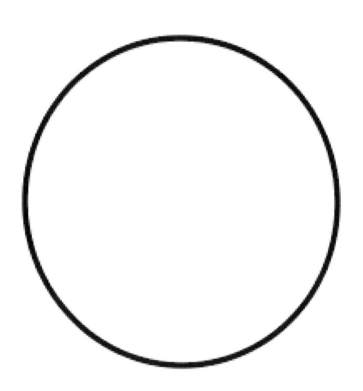

Yin and Yang

Mandalas

Look at nature and you will see all sorts of round shapes – the earth, moon, planets, orbits, flowers and so on. Mandalas were created in ancient times with religions and spirituality and with rich tradition. Suffice it to say that creating or coloring

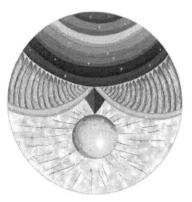 in a mandala is quite soothing and allows one to focus better, as well as to calm the spirit.

Mandalas are not difficult to make and there is no right or wrong about them. Just use your imagination to fill in the circle on the next page (your creation) or on the following page you will find a free mandala from the web which you can color in to your heart's content.

Mandala

Mandala to Color

Labyrinth

You didn't realize you already know about labyrinths, did you? Think back on those times you did a maze. Yep, that's kind of what a labyrinth is. A labyrinth *walk* can be amazingly calming. Without taking the time to chalk out or mark a place outside in which to walk a labyrinth, create a path within your home and walk that listening to calming  music as you do so. But you can also create a maze to do sitting down at your desk. Of course, I think both methods are effective, although my preference is to walk the labyrinth.

Labyrinth

Create Your Own Labyrinth

Scribble Drawing

Sometimes it feels just healthy to take a pen or pencil or crayon and scribble. Slow down, close your eyes and allow your pencil to guide you. When you are finished, look at the scribble and see if you can see anything. Color it in! This works especially

well if you just feel stuck and don't know what to draw or what kind of art to create. It's freeing and fun. And, who knows? It might be something pleasing to look at in the end.

Scribble Drawing

Scribble Drawing

Story Boards

In narrative therapy, counselors help clients understand the story of their lives. Those stories can only be told by the client and when completed, it can be viewed as a documentary of how something happened. You can make a story board for something that is perplexing you with images and/or text. Some people find that using the computer works best while using images from free programs of clip art.

This method also helps in externalizing information about our lives that allows us to become more objective in solving problems.

Story Board

Story Board

Crayon Resist

Ever wonder how something so bleak and dark can be used to uncover something quite beautiful? The crayon resist idea is available commercially (scratch

 art), but it is more fun to create your own product. Simply place a few brightly colored marks on a sheet of paper and then color over with black, covering all the color.

Then with a sharp pointed instrument, start removing some of the black. You will end up

with a pleasing project.

Crayon Resist

Crayon Resist

Tissue Art

Using a variety of media, you can create a visually pleasing picture using watercolors and tissue paper. First cut out any shapes you'd like. Put those aside and take your brush and paint a background for those items. When the background is dry, lightly glue the tissue to the page. When dry, you can paint

over with a complementary color.

You can use light colors or darker, more vibrant colors,

depending on your mood. Adding black pen final touches allows the pictures to pop.

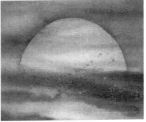

Tissue Art

Tissue Art

Appendix II

Sometimes it takes a while to work out the stress and trauma of the world. Trying some of these long term activities may assist in creating more harmony in your life.

Balancing Your Life

Research has documented that medication plus therapy is useful in obtaining the best possible mental wellness in individuals. This wellness comes at a price. It is not instantaneous as most of us would like to believe. Just take a pill and instant curative experience. Not gonna happen. It takes months and sometimes even years to heal. The following are some activities that might supplement your healing process. It might even help you keep your equilibrium on an even keel.

Scrapbooking

With the increase in digital technology, scrapbooking has become increasingly easier to do. Some people prefer a solitary experience, while others love to get together with friends and create.

 Be sure to allow yourself enough time to get materials out and accomplish at least one page per session. My friend does a wonderful job of documenting her many trips and when feeling down, takes the time to add to them or just view them. My mother in law scrapbooked 75 years ago. For something to last that long, you know it had to serve some greater purpose.

Scrapbooking can be just a journal page and a photo or a

magazine picture. Or it can be fancy, with lettering and stickers. It can be commercially made materials or just a few sheets of paper you have stapled together and use as your scrapbook.

Any way you look at it, scrapbooking allows you to organize memorabilia in a neat and focused manner.

Altered Books

Altered books, when googled, pop up in the hundreds. Artists world-wide are creating new pieces of art, using discarded books. Initially, it

bothered me to destroy a book, but when I read the title and saw that it was headed to the dump, I felt better about my choice of using it for art. My beloved mother-in-law loved altering books with her sister in the 1930s! They took recipes, invitations, and newspaper

clippings and glued them into old books.

Today's altered book artist can do the same, leaving the cover as is, or totally renovate the book with art and painting right onto pages. Some artists choose to cut out part of the book, allowing there to be a place to save something valuable. Others use

the recycled book as a scrapbook. Whatever venue
 you choose, the altered
book will take you
places in your mind you
only thought about
before.

Book Clubs

Oprah's book club epitomizes the best of social book learning. After reading a book, it is not only

helpful, but more gratifying to discuss the book with others. Some people decide on a book and then meet once a month to discuss it.

Others make it a night out with dinner, discussion, and a bit of wine. Whatever venue you choose, reading good books and talking about them

with others is extremely edifying as well as emotionally healthy.

As a former English teacher, I can honestly say that book reports can be so very boring and mundane, but having book groups sharing and creating

183

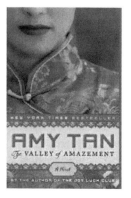

something – now that makes it worth your time. One example might be to read a book about a certain culture (and, yes, fiction is great) and then have a themed dinner or some food, music, or art from that culture shared with friends. Play music from that culture. Watch a video from that land.... Your imagination is your only limit.

Painting Parties

A recent rage in the Northwest (and I am assuming throughout the nation) is hosting a Paint Party, where folks gather in a home, bar, restaurant or other venue, and paint with the lead of a hired artist. Prices vary from $25 in my city to over $50 per person in larger cities.

The event serves to give confidence to those who consider themselves non-artists and a place to enjoy the company of other like-minded individuals.

Maxine of **www.PaintnPartyOr.com** hosts parties at local restaurants and in homes and is very enthusiastic about helping others enjoy art. Art and celebration have become synonymous in her neck of the woods.

Communities around the nation are boasting their own version of paint parties – check with your local art organization to see if they can put you in touch with one. You will find that art making reduces stress, anxiety, and allows one to focus. Not bad traits for an evening or afternoon of fun.

End Notes

Many books exist that give a person ideas on how to draw, paint, and/or sculpt. The internet is filled with ideas – if you want to learn how to draw eyes, for example, several sites offer tutorials complete with video instruction.

The expressive arts are a must in our society – they take away the dull and mundane and provide excitement, color, and soul to this journey we call life.

May you fill your moments with tidbits of art, music, drama, and dance!

Printed in Great Britain
by Amazon.co.uk, Ltd.,
Marston Gate.